# Super Scarves to knit

All the rage in fashion circles, super-sized scarves are the ultimate versatile accessory for women and men alike. Each of the six knit designs in this book is about 14 inches wide and 120 inches long, offering luxurious warmth and style.

LEISURE ARTS, INC. • Maumelle, Arkansas

# PEBBLES

BEGINNER

**Finished Size:** 13" x 120" (33 cm x 305 cm)

## SHOPPING LIST

**Yarn** (Bulky Weight) 5 BULKY

[5 ounces, 153 yards (140 grams, 140 meters) per skein]:

- ☐ 6 skeins

**Knitting Needles**

- ☐ Straight, size 10½ (6.5 mm) **or** size needed for gauge

## GAUGE INFORMATION

In pattern,

12 sts (2 repeats) = 3¼" (8.25 cm),

16 rows = 3½" (9 cm)

## SCARF

Cast on 48 sts.

**Row 1** (Right side)**:** (P2, K4) across.

**Row 2:** (P4, K2) across.

**Rows 3 and 4:** Repeat Rows 1 and 2.

**Row 5:** K2, P2, (K4, P2) across to last 2 sts, K2.

**Row 6:** P2, K2, (P4, K2) across to last 2 sts, P2.

**Rows 7 and 8:** Repeat Rows 5 and 6.

**Row 9:** (K4, P2) across.

**Row 10:** (K2, P4) across.

**Rows 11 and 12:** Repeat Rows 9 and 10.

Repeat Rows 1-12 for pattern until Scarf measures approximately 120" (305 cm) from cast on edge, ending by working Row 4, 8, **or** 12.

Bind off all sts in pattern.

# RADIANCE

EASY

**Finished Size:** 13½" x 120"
(34.5 cm x 305 cm)

## SHOPPING LIST

### Yarn (Medium Weight) MEDIUM 4

[3.5 ounces, 270 yards
(100 grams, 247 meters) per skein]:
☐ 5 skeins

### Knitting Needles

Straight,
☐ Size 8 (5 mm) **and**
☐ Size 9 (5.5 mm)
**or** sizes needed for gauge

## GAUGE INFORMATION

With larger size needles, in pattern,
16 sts (2 repeats) = 3¼" (8.25 cm),
16 rows = 2½" (6.25 cm)

## SCARF

With smaller size needles, cast on 66 sts.

**Rows 1-8** (Border)**:** Knit across.

Change to larger size needles.

**Row 9** (Right side)**:** ★ K5, slip 3 as if to **purl** wyif (with yarn in front); repeat from ★ across to last 10 sts, K 10.

**Row 10:** K5, P4, K3, (P5, K3) across to last 6 sts, P1, K5.

**Row 11:** K6, slip 3 as if to **purl** wyif, ★ K5, slip 3 as if to **purl** wyif; repeat from ★ across to last 9 sts, K9.

**Row 12:** K5, P3, K3, (P5, K3) across to last 7 sts, P2, K5.

**Row 13:** K7, slip 3 as if to **purl** wyif, ★ K5, slip 3 as if to **purl** wyif; repeat from ★ across to last 8 sts, K8.

**Row 14:** K5, P2, K3, (P5, K3) across to last 8 sts, P3, K5.

**Row 15:** K8, slip 3 as if to **purl** wyif, ★ K5, slip 3 as if to **purl** wyif; repeat from ★ across to last 7 sts, K7.

**Row 16:** K5, P1, K3, (P5, K3) across to last 9 sts, P4, K5.

**Row 17:** K9, slip 3 as if to **purl** wyif, ★ K5, slip 3 as if to **purl** wyif; repeat from ★ across to last 6 sts, K6.

**Row 18:** K8, P5, (K3, P5) across to last 5 sts, K5.

**Row 19:** K 10, ★ slip 3 as if to **purl** wyif, K5; repeat from ★ across.

**Row 20:** K7, P5, (K3, P5) across to last 6 sts, K6.

**Row 21:** K5, slip 1 as if to **purl** wyif, K5, ★ slip 3 as if to **purl** wyif, K5; repeat from ★ across to last 7 sts, slip 2 as if to **purl** wyif, K5.

**Row 22:** K6, P5, (K3, P5) across to last 7 sts, K7.

**Row 23:** K5, slip 2 as if to **purl** wyif, K5, ★ slip 3 as if to **purl** wyif, K5; repeat from ★ across to last 6 sts, slip 1 as if to **purl** wyif, K5.

**Row 24:** K5, P5, (K3, P5) across to last 8 sts, K8.

Repeat Rows 9-24 for pattern until Scarf measures approximately 119" (302.5 cm) from cast on edge, ending by working a **wrong** side row.

Change to smaller size needles.

**Last 8 Rows** (Border)**:** Knit across.

Bind off all sts in **knit**.

# REGENCY

EASY

**Finished Size:** 14" x 120"
(35.5 cm x 305 cm)

## SHOPPING LIST

**Yarn** (Super Bulky Weight)
[5 ounces, 81 yards
(142 grams, 74 meters) per skein]:
☐ 9 skeins

**Knitting Needles**
☐ Straight, size 13 (9 mm)
**or** size needed for gauge

## GAUGE INFORMATION

In pattern,
12 sts (2 repeats) = 4½" (11.5 cm),
12 rows (1 repeat) = 4" (10 cm)

## STITCH GUIDE

**KNIT 2 TOGETHER**
***(abbreviated K2 tog)***

Insert the right needle into the front of the first two stitches on the left needle as if to **knit** ***(Fig. A)***, then knit them together as if they were one stitch.

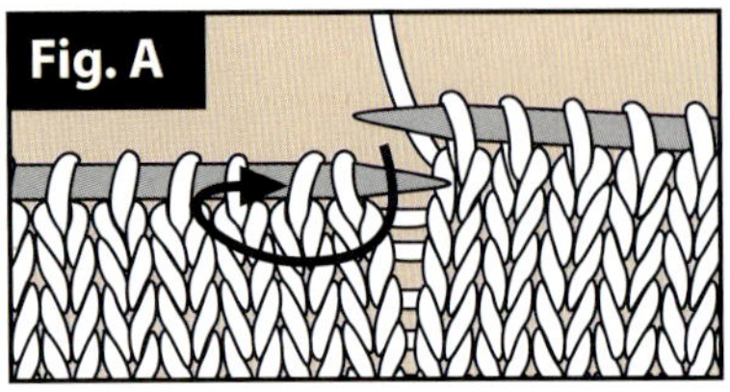

Fig. A

**SLIP 1, KNIT 2 TOGETHER, PASS SLIPPED STITCH OVER**
***(abbreviated slip 1, K2 tog, PSSO)***

Slip one stitch as if to **knit**, then knit the next two stitches together ***(Fig. A)***. With the left needle, bring the slipped stitch over the stitch just made ***(Fig. B)*** and off the needle.

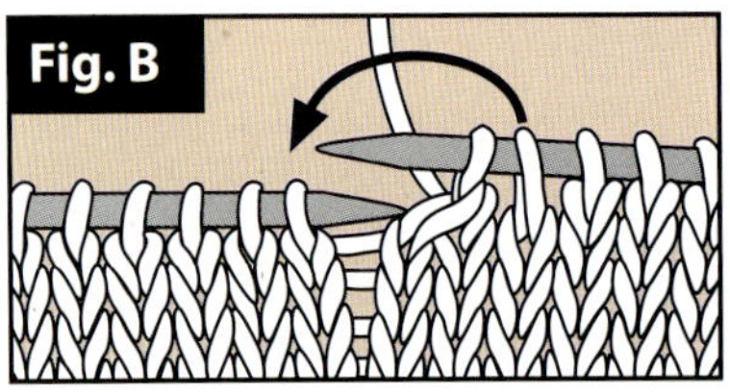

Fig. B

## SCARF

Cast on 37 sts.

**Row 1** (Right side)**:** K1, (P1, K1) across.

**Row 2:** P1, (K1, P1) across.

**Row 3:** K1, P1, K3, (P3, K3) across to last 2 sts, P1, K1.

**Row 4:** P1, K1, P3, (K3, P3) across to last 2 sts, K1, P1.

**Rows 5 and 6:** Repeat Rows 3 and 4.

**Row 7:** K1, P1, YO ***(Figs. 1a-c, page 15)***, slip 1 as if to **knit**, K2 tog, PSSO, YO, ★ K3, YO, slip 1 as if to **knit**, K2 tog, PSSO, YO; repeat from ★ across to last 2 sts, P1, K1.

**Row 8:** P1, K1, purl across to last 2 sts, K1, P1.

**Row 9:** K1, P4, K3, (P3, K3) across to last 5 sts, P4, K1.

**Row 10:** P1, K4, P3, (K3, P3) across to last 5 sts, K4, P1.

**Rows 11 and 12:** Repeat Rows 9 and 10.

**Row 13:** K1, P1, K3, ★ YO, slip 1 as if to **knit**, K2 tog, PSSO, YO, K3; repeat from ★ across to last 2 sts, P1, K1.

**Row 14:** P1, K1, purl across to last 2 sts, K1, P1.

Repeat Rows 3-14 for pattern until Scarf measures approximately 119½" (303.5 cm) from cast on edge, ending by working Row 8.

**Next Row:** K1, (P1, K1) across.

**Last Row:** P1, (K1, P1) across.

Bind off all sts in pattern.

# REVERSIBLE CABLES

EASY +

**Finished Size:** 14¼" x 120" (36 cm x 305 cm)

## SHOPPING LIST

### Yarn (Bulky Weight) 5

[3.5 ounces, 153 yards (100 grams, 139.9 meters) per skein]:

☐ 9 skeins

### Knitting Needles

☐ Straight, size 11 (8 mm) **or** size needed for gauge

### Additional Supplies

☐ Cable needle

## GAUGE INFORMATION

In pattern,

18 sts (1 repeat) = 3½" (9 cm),

16 rows = 4" (10 cm)

## STITCH GUIDE

**CABLE** (uses 12 sts)

Slip next 6 sts onto cable needle and hold in **front** of work, (K1, P1) 3 times from left needle, (K1, P1) 3 times from cable needle.

## SCARF

Cast on 75 sts.

**Row 1** (Right side)**:** Slip 1 as if to **knit**, P1, ★ K1, P2, K1, (P1, K1) 5 times, P2, K1, P1; repeat from ★ across to last st, K1.

**Row 2:** Slip 1 as if to **purl**, K1, ★ P1, K2, P1, (K1, P1) 5 times, K2, P1, K1; repeat from ★ across to last st, P1.

**Rows 3 and 4:** Repeat Rows 1 and 2.

**Row 5:** Slip 1 as if to **knit**, P1, K1, ★ P2, work Cable, (P1, K1) twice; repeat from ★ across.

**Rows 6-14:** Repeat Row 2, then repeat Rows 1 and 2, 4 times.

Repeat Rows 5-14 for pattern until Scarf measures approximately 120" (305 cm) from cast on edge, ending by working Row 6.

Bind off all sts in pattern.

# CHEVRON

EASY +

**Finished Size:** 13¾" x 120" (35 cm x 305 cm)

## SHOPPING LIST

### Yarn (Medium Weight) 4

[5 ounces, 245 yards (140 grams, 224 meters) per skein]:

☐ 5 skeins self striping yarn

### Knitting Needles

☐ Straight, size 9 (5.5 mm) **or** size needed for gauge

## GAUGE INFORMATION

In pattern,
12 sts (1 repeat) = 2½" (6.25 cm),
24 rows (1 repeat) = 3¾" (9.5 cm)

## STITCH GUIDE

**SLIP 2, KNIT 1, PASS 2 STITCHES OVER** ***(abbreviated slip 2, K1, P2SSO)*** (uses 3 sts)

Insert right needle in first 2 sts on left needle as if to **knit** and slip them together onto right needle, K1, pass both slipped sts over knit st ***(Fig. A)***.

**Fig. A**

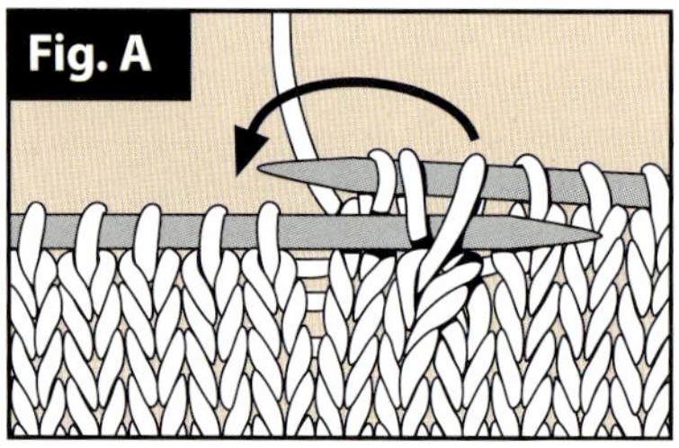

## SCARF

Cast on 66 sts.

**Rows 1-6** (Border)**:** Knit across.

**Row 7** (Right side)**:** K3, ★ YO ***(Fig. 1a, page 15)***, K4, slip 2, K1, P2SSO, K4, YO, K1; repeat from ★ across to last 3 sts, K3.

**Row 8:** K3, purl across to last 3 sts, K3.

**Rows 9-20:** Repeat Rows 7 and 8, 6 times.

**Row 21:** K3, ★ YO, K4, slip 2, K1, P2SSO, K4, YO, K1; repeat from ★ across to last 3 sts, K3.

**Rows 22-24:** Knit across.

Repeat Rows 7-24 for pattern until Scarf measures approximately 119" (302.5 cm) from cast on edge, ending by working Row 21.

**Last 5 Rows** (Border)**:** Knit across.

Bind off all sts in **knit**.

# MOSAIC

INTERMEDIATE

**Finished Size:** 13¾" x 120" (35 cm x 305 cm)

## SHOPPING LIST

**Yarn** (Bulky Weight) BULKY 5
[3.5 ounces, 127 yards (100 grams, 116 meters) per skein]:

- ☐ Main Color (Red) - 5 skeins
- ☐ Contrasting Color (Black) - 6 skeins

**Knitting Needles**

- ☐ Straight, size 10½ (6.5 mm) **or** size needed for gauge

## GAUGE INFORMATION

In pattern,
12 sts (1 repeat) = 3¼" (8.25 cm),
24 rows (1 repeat) = 3½" (9 cm)

Alternate working two rows of each color, carrying unused yarn along the edge. Slipping a stitch combines two colors that look like you changed colors.

When instructed to slip a stitch, always slip as if to **purl**. On **right** side rows, hold yarn in **back** and on **wrong** side rows, hold yarn in **front**.

## SCARF

With Main Color, cast on 51 sts.

**Rows 1 and 2:** Knit across.

**Row 3** (Right side)**:** With Contrasting Color, K1, slip 1, (K 11, slip 1) across to last st, K1.

**Row 4 AND ALL WRONG SIDE ROWS:** Knit the same color sts and slip all of the slipped sts.

**Row 5:** With Main Color, K4, slip 1, (K1, slip 1) 3 times, ★ K5, slip 1, (K1, slip 1) 3 times; repeat from ★ across to last 4 sts, K4.

**Row 7:** With Contrasting Color, K3, ★ slip 1, K7, slip 1, K3; repeat from ★ across.

**Row 9:** With Main Color, K2, slip 1, K3, slip 1, ★ K1, slip 1, K3, slip 1; repeat from ★ across to last 2 sts, K2.

**Row 11:** With Contrasting Color, K5, slip 1, K3, slip 1, ★ K7, slip 1, K3, slip 1; repeat from ★ across to last 5 sts, K5.

**Row 13:** With Main Color, K2, slip 1, K1, slip 1, K5, slip 1, ★ (K1, slip 1) 3 times, K5, slip 1; repeat from ★ across to last 4 sts, K1, slip 1, K2.

**Row 15:** With Contrasting Color, K7, slip 1, (K 11, slip 1) across to last 7 sts, K7.

**Row 17:** With Main Color, K2, slip 1, K1, slip 1, K5, slip 1, ★ (K1, slip 1) 3 times, K5, slip 1; repeat from ★ across to last 4 sts, K1, slip 1, K2..

**Row 19:** With Contrasting Color, K5, slip 1, K3, slip 1, ★ K7, slip 1, K3, slip 1; repeat from ★ across to last 5 sts, K5.

**Row 21:** With Main Color, K2, slip 1, K3, slip 1, ★ K1, slip 1, K3, slip 1; repeat from ★ across to last 2 sts, K2.

**Row 23:** With Contrasting Color, K3, ★ slip 1, K7, slip 1, K3; repeat from ★ across.

**Row 25:** With Main Color, K4, slip 1, (K1, slip 1) 3 times, ★ K5, slip 1, (K1, slip 1) 3 times; repeat from ★ across to last 4 sts, K4.

**Row 27:** With Contrasting Color, K1, slip 1, (K 11, slip 1) across to last st, K1.

Repeat Rows 4-27 for pattern until Scarf measures approximately 119" (302.5 cm) from cast on edge, ending by working Row 16.

Cut Contrasting Color.

**Last 2 Rows:** With Main Color, knit across.

Bind off all sts as if to **knit**.

# GENERAL INSTRUCTIONS

## ABBREVIATIONS

| | |
|---|---|
| cm | centimeters |
| K | knit |
| mm | millimeters |
| P | purl |
| PSSO | pass slipped stitch over |
| P2SSO | pass 2 slipped stitches over |
| st(s) | stitch(es) |
| tog | together |
| wyif | with yarn in front |
| YO | yarn over |

## SYMBOLS & TERMS

★ — work instructions following ★ as many **more** times as indicated in addition to the first time.

( ) or [ ] — work enclosed instructions **as many** times as specified by the number immediately following **or** contains explanatory remarks.

## GAUGE

Exact gauge is **essential** for proper size. Before beginning your project, make a sample swatch in the yarn and needles specified in the individual instructions. After completing the swatch, measure it, counting your stitches and rows carefully. If your swatch is larger or smaller than specified, **make another, changing needle size to get the correct gauge.** Keep trying until you find the size needles that will give you the specified gauge.

| Yarn Weight Symbol & Names | LACE 0 | SUPER FINE 1 | FINE 2 | LIGHT 3 | MEDIUM 4 | BULKY 5 | SUPER BULKY 6 | JUMBO 7 |
|---|---|---|---|---|---|---|---|---|
| Type of Yarns in Category | Fingering, size 10 crochet thread | Sock, Fingering, Baby | Sport, Baby | DK, Light Worsted | Worsted, Afghan, Aran | Chunky, Craft, Rug | Super Bulky, Roving | Jumbo, Roving |
| Knit Gauge Ranges in Stockinette St to 4" (10 cm) | 33-40 sts** | 27-32 sts | 23-26 sts | 21-24 sts | 16-20 sts | 12-15 sts | 7-11 sts | 6 sts and fewer |
| Advised Needle Size Range | 000 to 1 | 1 to 3 | 3 to 5 | 5 to 7 | 7 to 9 | 9 to11 | 11 to 17 | 17 and larger |

* GUIDELINES ONLY: The chart above reflects the most commonly used gauges and needle sizes for specific yarn categories.

** Lace weight yarns are usually knitted on larger needles to create lacy openwork patterns. Accordingly, a gauge range is difficult to determine. Always follow the gauge stated in your pattern.

| KNIT TERMINOLOGY | | |
|---|---|---|
| UNITED STATES | | INTERNATIONAL |
| gauge | = | tension |
| bind off | = | cast off |
| yarn over (YO) | = | yarn forward (yfwd) **or** yarn around needle (yrn) |

| KNITTING NEEDLES | | | | | | | | | | | | | | | | | | |
|---|---|---|---|---|---|---|---|---|---|---|---|---|---|---|---|---|---|---|
| U.S. | 0 | 1 | 2 | 3 | 4 | 5 | 6 | 7 | 8 | 9 | 10 | 10½ | 11 | 13 | 15 | 17 | 19 | 35 | 50 |
| U.K. | 13 | 12 | 11 | 10 | 9 | 8 | 7 | 6 | 5 | 4 | 3 | 2 | 1 | 00 | 000 | --- | --- | --- | --- |
| Metric - mm | 2 | 2.25 | 2.75 | 3.25 | 3.5 | 3.75 | 4 | 4.5 | 5 | 5.5 | 6 | 6.5 | 8 | 9 | 10 | 12.75 | 15 | 19 | 25 |

| | |
|---|---|
| **BEGINNER** | Projects for first-time knitters using basic knit and purl stitches. Minimal shaping. |
| **EASY** | Projects using basic stitches, repetitive stitch patterns, simple color changes, and simple shaping and finishing. |
| **INTERMEDIATE** | Projects with a variety of stitches, such as basic cables and lace, simple intarsia, double-pointed needles and knitting in the round needle techniques, mid-level shaping and finishing. |
| **EXPERIENCED** | Projects using advanced techniques and stitches, such as short rows, fair isle, more intricate intarsia, cables, lace patterns, and numerous color changes. |

## YARN OVER

### After a knit stitch, before a knit stitch

Bring the yarn forward between the needles, then back over the top of the right hand needle, so that it is now in position to knit the next stitch *(Fig. 1a)*.

Fig. 1a

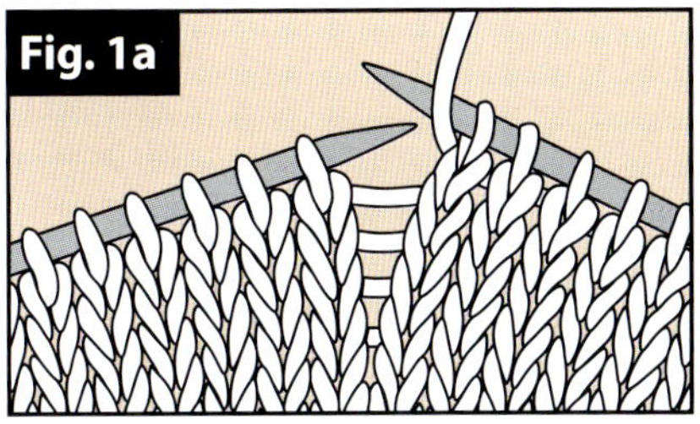

### After a knit stitch, before a purl stitch

Bring the yarn forward between the needles, then back over the top of the right hand needle and forward between the needles again, so that it is now in position to purl the next stitch *(Fig. 1b)*.

Fig. 1b

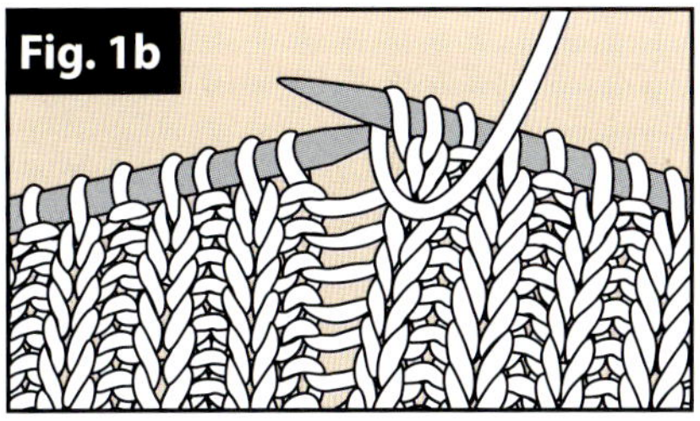

### After a purl stitch, before a knit stitch

Take the yarn over the right hand needle to the back, so that it is now in position to knit the next stitch *(Fig. 1c)*.

Fig. 1c

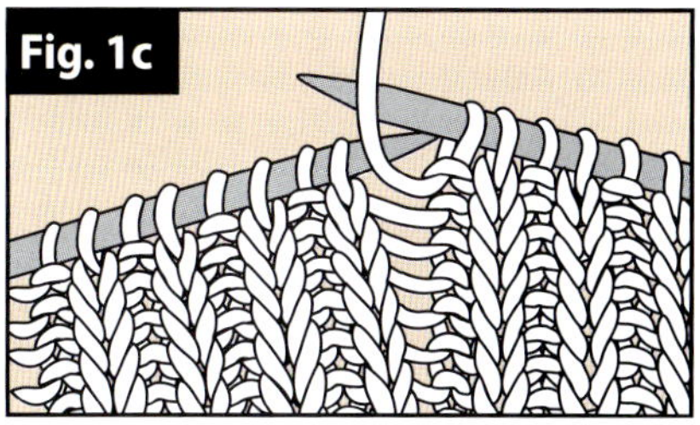

## Meet Lisa Gentry

A native of Germany who now resides in Louisiana, Lisa Gentry has been a crocheter since first grade. She came to the attention of the yarn industry after being awarded the title of Fastest Crocheter by the Guinness World Records in 2005. She was also later named America's fastest knitter by the Craft Yarn Council.

Since then, her knit and crochet designs have been prominently featured in top magazines and published in nearly 30 Leisure Arts books. Topics include crocodile stitch, chain knitting (a technique Lisa invented), ribbon crochet, women's sweaters, celebrity baby fashions, slouchy beanies for the family, urban hats knit with The Knook, cowls, neckwear, and more.

Find Lisa's books on LeisureArts.com. For more about her designs, visit Ravelry.com and her company website, HookAndNeedleDesigns.com.

# YARN INFORMATION

The Scarves in this book were made using a variety of yarns. Any brand of the specified weight yarn may be used. It is best to refer to the yardage/meters when determining how many balls or skeins to purchase. Remember, to arrive at the finished size, it is the GAUGE/TENSION that is important, not the brand of yarn.

For your convenience, listed below are the yarns used to create our photography models. Because yarn manufacturers make frequent changes in their product lines, you may sometimes find it necessary to use a substitute yarn or to search for the discontinued product at alternate suppliers (locally or online).

**PEBBLES**
*Lion Brand® Wool-Ease® Chunky*
#155 Silver Grey

**RADIANCE**
*Red Heart® Unforgettable®*
#3977 Sunrise

**REGENCY**
*Lion Brand® Hometown USA®*
#159 Madison Mustard

**REVERSIBLE CABLES**
*Premier® Downton Abbey Branson™*
#07 Oatmeal Cream

**CHEVRON**
*Premier® Sweet Roll™*
#14 Punch Pop

**MOSAIC**
*Lion Brand® Lion's Pride® Woolspun®*
Main Color - #113 Red
Contrasting Color - #153 Black

We have made every effort to ensure that these instructions are accurate and complete. We cannot, however, be responsible for human error, typographical mistakes, or variations in individual work.

Production Team: Instructional/Technical Editor - Cathy Hardy; Editorial Writer - Susan Frantz Wiles; Senior Graphic Artist - Lora Puls; Graphic Artist - Victoria Temple; Photo Stylist - Lori Wenger; and Photographer - Jason Masters.